TALK,
PLAY,
AND
READ
WITH ME
MOMMY

TALK, PLAY, AND READ WITH ME MOMMY

Interactive Activities to
Enhance Your Child's
Language Development
From Birth to Age Five

JO ANN GRAMLICH, M.S.

authorHOUSE®

AuthorHouse™ LLC
1663 Liberty Drive
Bloomington, IN 47403
www.authorhouse.com
Phone: 1-800-839-8640

Published by AuthorHouse   05/27/2014

ISBN: 978-1-4490-6512-6 (sc)
ISBN: 978-1-4490-6513-3 (e)

Library of Congress Control Number: 2014900907

Table of Contents

Games for Toddlers

1 to 1 ½ Years

1 ½ to 2 Years

Games for Preschoolers 71

Introduction

Early communication between you and your child is essential and begins as early as birth. It's important to know how to get your child ready for school long before their first ride on a school bus. This book will provide you with creative ideas to help enhance your child's language skills during the early years. It has many stimulating activities and games that are developmentally appropriate for infants, toddlers and preschoolers. There are animal games, musical sing-a-long games, counting and matching games, story time games, listening games and so much more. These games can be played when you and your child have a few extra minutes during daily routines, whenever you are on the go, or anytime you simply want to have fun together.

In addition, you will find developmental language milestones from birth to 5 years because so many language skills are acquired during this important expanding period in your child's life. A compilation of all the strategies and techniques I was taught and use with children in my workplace are also presented within the assorted activities and games included in this book.

Although children will acquire language at a different rate due to individual differences, your child can naturally learn and develop various communication skills from birth to age five. This development can take place within a language rich environment in conjunction with using specific techniques that will help encourage and stimulate your child's language growth. Good luck to you and your child as you interact together and remember to keep on talking!

Finally, many thanks go out to all the children who have brought so much joy into my life and who have given me the opportunity to pass along this little handbook of fun activities and games.

Developmental Language Milestones

Birth to 6 Months
Responds to voice and sound
Is calmed by familiar friendly voices
Repeats same sounds
Makes pleasure sounds, coos, or gurgles
Cries for hunger or other needs
Babbles or coos during vocal play
Smiles happily when spoken to
Recognizes voices
Laughs playfully
Produces /b/, /p/, & /m/ sounds when babbling
Uses sounds or gestures when in need
Vocalizes when engaged in self-initiated sound play

7 to 12 Months
Responds to and understands own name
Listens to new words and imitates sounds
Understands a few new words (e.g., mommy,
daddy, & bye bye)
Uses sounds and song-like patterns when babbling
Imitates sounds or intonation patterns produced by others
Listens when talked to
Begins to change babbling type speech to jargon
Likes simple nursery songs and rhymes

Produces first true words or word approximations
Understands simple commands
Imitates animal noises
Vocalizes playfully when left alone

1 to 1 ½ Years
Uses one or more words with meaning
Recognizes familiar objects, pictures, and people
Produces adult like intonation patterns
Understands simple commands given cues
Repeats and imitates words over and over again
Combines gestures, vocalizations, and words
Imitates words heard
Enjoys requesting items of interest
Identifies a few body parts
Uses many single word utterances
Begins to have 10 to 20 word vocabulary
Requests desired objects
Speech is 25% intelligible to the unfamiliar listener

1 ½ to 2 Years
Uses more words than jargon
Identifies 3 to 5 body parts
Follows simple directions without cues (e.g., come here and sit down)
Understands 300 words or more
Has an expressive vocabulary of 50-100 words
Begins to combine words together (2 word phrases)
Imitates two and three word utterances
Uses pronouns (I and me)
Listens to stories
Answers "what's that?" questions

Refers to self by name
Begins to follow two step directions
Names a few objects that are familiar
Speech is intelligible approximately 25-50% of the time
to the unfamiliar listener

2 to 2 ½ Years

Uses two and three word combinations
Points to action pictures in a book upon request
Points to pictures in a book when named
Asks questions using 1-2 words (e.g., Where baby?)
Enjoys participating in fingerplay songs and rhymes
Names common objects in environment
Has expressive vocabulary of 50-300 words
Understands concept of first and second person pronouns
(I and you)
Answers simple questions
Understands spatial concepts (in, out, off, on)
Requests familiar objects from environment
Identifies object by use
Says full name
Listens to simple stories
Speech is 50-65% intelligible

2 ½ to 3 Years

Uses 3 to 4 word sentences
Understands most things stated to him or her
Identifies objects by name and use
Has receptive vocabulary of 400-900 words
Follows simple 2 step commands
Identifies 7 to 8 body parts
Identifies part of an object (e.g., tail of a dog)
Answers "yes/no" & "what/where" questions

Asks what, where, and when questions
Has expressive vocabulary expanding to 900 words
Uses pronouns (I, me, you, mine & he and she emerging)
Takes turns during play routines
Carries on a conversation
Identifies 3 objects in a picture
Recites a few rhymes and fingerplay songs
Speech is 65-75% intelligible

3 to 4 Years
Follows 2 and 3 step commands
Has a receptive vocabulary of 1,000 words
Groups objects together (toys, animals, food)
Identifies pictures
Says full name, sex, and names street he/she lives on
Recites many nursery rhymes and songs
Answers most simple "wh" questions related to
activity at hand
Knows body parts on self
Has an expressive vocabulary of 900-1500 words
Asks who, what, where, and why questions
Uses 4 to 6 word sentences
Tells how objects are used
Repeats sentences
Uses verbs (is, are, and am) correctly in sentences
Uses pronouns (he, she, I, you, and mine) consistently
Uses more compound and complex sentences
with proper verb tenses
Speech is 80% intelligible

4 to 5 Years
Identifies colors (red, blue, yellow, and green)
Identifies shapes (circle, square, and triangle)

Listens to short stories and answers related questions

Has a receptive vocabulary of 1500-2500 words

Understands spatial concepts (in back of, next to, and in front of)

Understands complex directions (e.g., point to the small green ball in the box)

Understands quantity concepts (e.g., count the flowers or point to the pot with 4 flowers)

Counts to 10 by rote

Answers questions related to simple stories

Uses 4 to 8 word sentences

Has an expressive vocabulary of approximately 1000-2000 words

Uses grammatically correct sentences

Repeats complex sentences (6-9 words) when asked

Answers complex 2 part questions

Names familiar animals

Names common objects in picture books or magazines

Defines words by use (e.g., What is a chair?)

Speech is 90% intelligible

Sources: The information stated here was compiled from a variety of sources including American Speech-Language-Hearing Association (1997-2014); Bowen (1998); Kipping, Gard, Gilman, and Gorman (2012); and Rossetti (2005).

Games for Infants

Making Sounds

A caregiver can encourage a baby to imitate and respond to sounds and vocalizations.

Playing the Activity: Place your baby down on a padded flat surface with good support. As you lean over your baby, make eye contact and say something in an encouraging tone. Listen to your baby. Your baby will then respond with sounds. Imitate the sounds your baby makes. Your baby may smile so make sure you smile back and continue vocalizing.

Rattle Time

Encourage your baby to vocalize and listen by calling his attention to a toy, object, or your talking or singing voice.

Playing the Activity: Place your baby down on a flat surface such as a bed or padded floor. Simply gather some toys or objects that make calming sounds such as a rattle, soft bells, music box, or a cup with a spoon. Hold the object in front of your baby about eight to ten inches from his eyes. Shake the object (rattle) gently and move it in and out of your baby's sight. Smile and imitate any sounds (cooing or gurgling) your baby makes while you play the game together.

Gentle Voices

Your baby will love the sound of your sweet tender voice.

<u>Playing the Activity:</u> Hold your baby in your arms while making good eye contact. Begin to talk to your baby using a warm and tender gentle voice. You can talk about your baby's cute little face, body parts, or favorite little toys. As you talk, you may hear vowel-like, cooing, or gurgling sounds. Go ahead and repeat any vocalizations you hear.

Musical Sing-a-Long

Babies love listening to the gentle sounds of lullabies or nursery rhymes.

<u>Playing the Activity:</u> Hold your baby in front of you or on your lap. Look at your baby, face to face, as you sing or play a favorite lullaby such as "Twinkle, Twinkle, Little Star" or "Rock-a-Bye Baby." Make good eye contact with your baby. When your baby vocalizes or coos, repeat any of the sounds your baby makes during your musical sing-a-long. Continue singing to your baby.

Lots of Sounds

Your baby will hear you make all kinds of different sounds and enjoy repeating them back to you.

Playing the Activity: While holding your baby make good eye contact. As you look and talk to your baby, begin to laugh, whistle, or make non-speech sounds like humming or gurgling. If your baby repeats any of the sounds, talk about them. You can say, "You're gurgling little Lou Lou. I like the sounds you're making." Your baby may smile back at you, so remember to keep on making lots of sounds and vocalizations.

Pat-a-Cake

Infants enjoy this playful game because of the rhythmic sounds and simple rhymes.

Playing the Activity: Place your baby on your lap or in an infant seat. Take your baby's hands and clap them together as you say the "Pat-a-Cake" rhyme. Continue making the hand motions along with the rhymes. Be prepared to repeat the game several times.

> *Pat-a-cake, pat-a-cake, baker's man,* (clap baby's hands together)
> *Bake me a cake as fast as you can;*
> *Pat it and roll it* (roll baby's hands)
> *And mark it with a "B,"* (make initial on baby's tummy)
> *And put it in the oven for baby* (or say baby's first name) *and me!*

Tender Tickles

Your baby will enjoy the warm feeling of your tender touch.

Playing the Activity: Place your baby on a flat surface such as a bed or padded floor. Gently touch your baby's body parts such as the belly, arms, or legs in a circular motion with your fingertips. As you touch your baby's body parts name them. You can use different objects to touch your baby including a soft cloth, silky string, feather, or lace. Make good eye contact. If you hear any sounds, repeat them back to your baby.

Playful Reading

Reading is a fun way to "talk" with your baby. Your baby will not only listen to all sorts of different sounds, words, and rhythmic patterns, but will see all kinds of pictures too.

Playing the Activity: Hold your baby close to you while sitting comfortably on your lap. Select a book with simple colorful pictures and begin to point to them. As you point to the pictures, begin to name them and describe the pictures with a few words or phrases. Help your baby touch the pictures. If you hear any sounds or vocalizations from your baby, imitate them and smile back at your baby.

Merry Melodies

Babies love to hear you sing as you feed, change, play, or bathe them. As you sing simple lullabies, you will establish a special closeness and bond with your baby.

Playing the Activity: Hold your baby close to you while you look and smile back. Begin to sing a lullaby.

> *Row, row, row your boat*
> *Gently down the stream,*
> *Merrily, merrily, merrily, merrily,*
> *Life is but a dream.*

Your baby may smile back at you or try to sing along. Repeat any vocalizations or sounds your baby makes.

Peek-a-Boo

Babies love to participate in games where they learn to listen, take turns, and look at the people playing with them.

Playing the Activity: Place your baby on a padded flat surface or in an infant seat. Move your face in and out of your baby's visual range. Hide your face in back of your hands or in a blanket while suddenly showing your face to your baby and say, "Peek-a-boo, I see you!" Your baby will laugh and smile when looking at your face. Smile back and repeat the game.

Just Talk

Encourage your baby to talk while making random movements during daily routines.

Playing the Activity: As your baby is chewing on a squeeze toy, say, "mmm, mmm, mmm!" If your baby is bouncing in a swing, say, "Bounce, bounce, and bounce!" If your baby is drinking milk from a bottle, say, "M-m-m-milk." If your baby is playing with a rattle, say, "Shake, shake, and shake." Listen and imitate any sounds your baby makes.

Tubby Time

Bath time is a perfect time to name your baby's body parts and reinforce sounds and smiles that your baby makes as you gently splash the water together.

Playing the Activity: Place your baby in an upright position in the bathtub. While washing your baby, name some body parts. You can say in a sing-song tone, "This is the way we wash your tummy, wash your tummy, and wash your tummy." Continue washing other body parts while naming them and singing about them to your baby. Be sure to imitate any sounds your baby makes while playing "Tubby Time!"

So Big

Your baby will enjoy imitating you as you play interactive games.

Playing the Activity: Place your baby on a flat surface or in a supported high chair facing you. Begin showing your baby how to play "So Big" by placing your arms up in the air. Ask, "How big is Charlie?" Use your baby's name. Your baby may raise his hands and gesture "so big." If he needs help, raise his hands and arms up high and say, "so big." If he makes any sounds, imitate them.

You can say and add more sounds to the game like "baba, bobo" or "goo-goo, ga ga." Your baby may imitate your sounds. Remember to repeat them back. Make good eye contact with your baby. Enjoy playing the game. You will have so much fun watching your baby move his hands and arms up in the air while you're playing the game together. If you hear any sounds, imitate them and praise your baby for good talking!

What is It?

Your baby can learn about objects and their actions by exploring.

Playing the Activity: Place or sit your baby in a high chair and put some objects like a ball, teddy bear, or train in front of her. Pick up the ball. Roll it to your baby and say, "Sophie, here's the ball." Say, "Your turn." Help her pick up the ball and roll it. While rolling the ball, say, "baba ball. Here's the ball." Eventually your baby will try to repeat the sounds and associate the words with the objects.

Repeat this activity with the teddy bear and train. Pick up the train and as you push it, say, "Here's the choo-choo." If your baby makes any sounds like "oo-oo" or "ah- ah," say, "Yes, it is a choo-choo. A train says choo-choo!" Repeat any sounds your baby makes.

Music Time

Music is a great way to encourage communication. You and your baby can sing along, listen, or dance.

Playing the Activity: Turn on a lullaby song on your CD player or just listen to some songs on the radio. Sing along while gently dancing with your baby. If your baby makes sounds, repeat them in a sing-song type voice.

For more fun, clap your baby's hands together to the beat of the music. Keep on singing those songs and repeating the sounds you hear from your baby!

Pretend Phone Talk

Your baby will love to play with a toy telephone and talk into it. You may even begin to hear your baby making and imitating babbling sounds as you play.

Playing the Activity: Place or sit your baby on your lap or on a flat surface. Hold the toy phone to your ear and say "Hello, hello. Is (_say baby's name_) there?" Next, place the toy phone to your baby's ear and say, "Hello, hello (_baby's name_)." Repeat this a few times.

Take the phone and pretend to have a simple conversation while using your baby's name in a few short phrases. Finally, let your baby hold the phone and place the toy phone to your baby's ear. Your baby may begin to talk into the phone. You may hear consonant-vowel combinations like "mama" or "dada" or other babbling sounds. Praise your baby by saying, "Good talking!"

Sit 'n Splash

Your baby will make and imitate babbling sounds as he splashes in the water and plays with bath toys.

Playing the Activity: Place your baby in a baby bin, bathtub, or small baby pool. Make sure he is sitting in a secure upright position. Gather some bath toys such as squishy ocean animals, plastic boats, and pouring cups. Place a few toys in front of your baby and say, "Jeremy, here's the boat." Push the boat and say, "The boat goes *vroom-vroom!*" Help your baby hold the boat and show him how it moves in the water. Make sounds like "papapa" or "vrvrvr."

Next, take a duck and hand it to your baby. Say, "Look Jeremy, a duck. Put it in the water. Now the duck is floating." Help him make little waves with his hands so the duck floats up and down. Make sounds like "dadada" or "papapa" as your baby plays with the duck in the water. Help your baby pour water over the duck with the cup. Say, "Look Jeremy! The duck is all wet." Make the "kakaka" or "wawawa" sound as he pours water from the cup.

Remember to repeat any sounds your baby makes. You can even add more sounds and soon you will be hearing your baby babble more and more on his own. Have fun splashing in the water.

Pop the Bubble

Popping bubbles will excite your baby. Your baby will love watching the bubbles as they float in the air and hearing the gentle popping sounds they make.

Playing the Activity: Place your baby near to you. As you start blowing bubbles from a bubble wand, say, "Look Gracie." As she looks, point to the bubbles floating around her. Say, "Bubbles. Pop the bubbles." Help her pop a bubble and say, "Pop, pop, and pop." Repeat any sounds your baby makes and add more sounds. She may say "papa" as she tries to pop the bubble. Just add more sounds like "papababa" or "babapapa" to her responses.

She is trying to talk and soon you will hear true words. After you pop a bubble, ask, "Where did the bubble go?" You may hear your baby say "baba." Say, "Yes, baba bubbles." You can gesture with your hands up and say, "Bubbles are all gone. Bubbles popped." Have fun popping bubbles and imitate any babbling sounds you hear your baby make.

Five Little Monkeys

This is an exciting fingerplay song with entertaining beats and hand movements that you and your baby can enjoy together.

Playing the Activity: Place or sit your baby next to you on a flat surface or seated next to you on a couch or chair. Sing the "Five Little Monkeys" song to your baby while helping your baby with hand movements. Below are the words to the song and the actions in parentheses.

Five little monkeys jumping on the bed (Move five fingers in a bouncing position on baby's other hand)
One fell off and bumped his head. (Turn one finger down and then bump fist to head)
Mama called the doctor and the doctor said, (Pretend to dial a telephone)
No more monkeys jumping on the bed. (Use pointing finger as if to punish)

Four little monkeys jumping on the bed (Move four fingers in a bouncing position on baby's other hand)
One fell off and bumped his head. (Turn one finger down and then bump fist to head)
Mama called the doctor and the doctor said, (Pretend to dial a telephone)
No more monkeys jumping on the bed. (Use pointing finger as if to punish)

Three little monkeys jumping on the bed (Move three fingers in a bouncing position on baby's other hand)
One fell off and bumped his head. (Turn one finger down and then bump fist to head)
Mama called the doctor and the doctor said, (Pretend to dial a telephone)
No more monkeys jumping on the bed. (Use pointing finger as if to punish)

Two little monkeys jumping on the bed (Move two fingers in a bouncing position on baby's other hand)
One fell off and bumped his head. (Turn one finger down and then bump fist to head)
Mama called the doctor and the doctor said, (Pretend to dial a telephone)
No more monkeys jumping on the bed. (Use pointing finger as if to punish)

One little monkey jumping on the bed (Move one finger in a bouncing position on baby's other hand)
One fell off and bumped his head. (Turn one finger down and then bump fist to head)

Mama called the doctor and the doctor said, (Pretend to dial a telephone)
No more monkeys jumping on the bed. (Use pointing finger as if to punish)

Looking at Pictures

Your baby can learn so many new things as you point to brightly colored objects and toys in picture books.

<u>Playing the Activity:</u> Place or sit your baby on your lap as you read together. As you point to a picture of an object or toy, talk about what we do with it. Say, "Here is a telephone (point to the telephone). The telephone goes *ring, ring!* There is a red car Lucas (point to the car). It goes *vroom, vroom.*"

Continue looking at pictures together. "Look Lucas. See the train (point to the train)? It goes *choo-choo*." Imitate any sounds your baby makes. Praise your baby for the sounds you hear.

Finding Body Parts

Your baby will enjoy talking and learning about different body parts.

Playing the Activity: Place or sit your baby on a flat surface so your baby can look directly at you. Put your hands on your head and say, "Touch your head!" Gently help your baby do the same action. Continue placing your hands on different body parts. Help your baby find the same body parts as you including tummy, legs, arms, nose, eyes, and feet.

Encourage your baby to vocalize. Keep on talking to your baby while you both find body parts and perform the actions together. Imitate any babbling sounds your baby makes.

Talking Time

Rocking or sitting in a chair as you hold your baby on your lap is a great way for you to talk and listen to your little one. Don't be surprised if you hear some sounds or words. Babies love to talk!

Playing the Activity: Place your baby on your lap as you sit down on a chair or rocking chair. As you begin to talk, use a soft and friendly voice. Look and smile at your baby and she will look back at you. You may begin to hear many different sounds, syllables, or words.

As you listen, repeat anything you hear your baby say as if you are having a conversation. Pause for a moment to let her vocalize. You may hear something like "baba" or "dada." If your baby says sounds like "baba" repeat the sounds she makes. Say, "bababab," and "Yes, Chloe, baba, baby."

Be creative and repeat babbling sounds back to your baby as if they were true words. Have fun and keep on talking!

Where Did It Go?

Your baby will soon begin to understand that objects exist even when the objects are out of sight.

Playing the Activity: Place or sit your baby on the floor and show him some toys such as a ball, a car, a teddy bear, or a train. Prompt your baby to pick up one toy and play with it for a few minutes. Let him know that you want a turn by saying, "It's my turn." Next, pick up a toy and hide it with a cloth. Help Johnny find the toy by asking, "Where's the ball?" Praise him if he finds the ball and repeat the game with another favorite toy.

Your baby will probably get excited and make sounds. You may even begin to hear word approximations or even a true word here or there. Remember to repeat and expand on your baby's sounds or words as you play together.

It Goes Up and Down

Your baby will have a lot of fun stacking objects and watching them tumble down to the floor. You can teach her to understand and say simple words like *up, down, on,* and *off.*

Playing the Activity: Place or sit your baby on the floor next to you and put different shaped blocks in front of her. Help your baby stack the blocks one-by-one to form a tower. Say, "Ally, look at the blocks." As you are stacking the blocks say, "Up, up, up." You may hear your baby repeat sounds or words. Praise her. When your tower is complete, knock it down while your baby is watching. Encourage her to say "down" as the blocks fall down. Repeat this several times.

Again, prompt your baby to stack the blocks up and knock them down by herself. Imitate any sounds, word approximations, or true words you hear and praise your baby for good talking.

Games for Toddlers

Can You Name It?

Your toddler will begin to use real words when communicating with you. You can help him produce sounds, words approximations, or true words by prompting him to talk during daily routines.

Playing the Activity: Place or sit your toddler down at a table for a snack. During snack time say, "Tommy, here's some juice. Can you tell me what it is?" Prompt him to say "juice." If he says "juju," say, "Yes, juice. You're drinking juice." Praise him. Other daily routines will allow you to prompt your toddler to talk.

During playtime, say, "Look Tommy, here's your ball. Can you say ball?" If he says "ba" or "ball," say, "bababa" or "ball. Yes, it is a ball," and praise him. He will soon say some true words on his own.

While reading him a story, say, "Here's your book. Do you see the puppy?" Point to the picture and ask, "What is it?" If he says the sound "pu," say, "pupupu" or "Yes, it is a puppy." Praise him for any sounds, word approximations, or true words you hear.

Imitate Me and See

Your toddler will love imitating anything and everything you do.

Playing the Activity: Sit on the floor with your toddler and say, "Imani, I'm clapping my hands (clap your hands). I'm touching my belly (touch your belly). I'm patting my arm (pat your arm)." You can add other toys and body movements to your game including tapping some objects together, waving your arms, stomping your feet, or shaking your head (yes/no).

Give your toddler a few seconds to observe what you are doing. Ask her to imitate you by waving her hands or stomping her feet. You may hear some sounds or true words coming from your toddler. Imitate them and keep on talking together as you play "Imitate Me and See!"

Take a Walk with Me

Your toddler will enjoy walking outside in your backyard or in the neighborhood. You can teach him about different things you will see during your walk together.

Playing the Activity: Ask your toddler to go for a walk. Say, "Robbie, please get your coat and hat." Help your toddler to get ready. Say, "You are going for a walk outside with me." As you begin, look around the neighborhood with your toddler and point to different things you see. He will love looking at the trees, flowers, insects, and birds. If you see a bird say, "Look at the bird. A bird says *chirp, chirp.*" Prompt him to say "bird."

Praise him for any sounds, word approximations, or true words heard. Continue to have your toddler point to different things he sees outside and talk with him about them.

Mirror Games

Your toddler will love gazing at herself in front of a mirror. She will become more aware of how to move her body. You can listen to her as she talks and looks at herself in the mirror.

Playing the Activity: Place your toddler in front of the mirror. Say, "Look. Sadie is in front of the mirror." Start to make funny faces and after each funny face ask your toddler to do the same. Watch as she imitates you. If you hear sounds or words, repeat them and praise her. Point out different body parts and imitate your toddler's movements. If she touches her tummy, say, "Yes, that's your tummy." Encourage her to say "tummy." Expand on your toddler's utterance by saying, "Yes, it is your little tummy. You have a cute little tummy. Tickle, Tickle!"

You can even find a favorite stuffed animal or doll and put it in front of the mirror. As you hold it, make it move and pretend to make it talk. Encourage your toddler to continue moving different body parts and talking as she looks in the mirror.

Animal Sounds

Your toddler will enjoy looking, playing, and learning about animals and the sounds they make.

<u>Playing the Activity:</u> Group together some toy animals. Pick out an animal and show it to your toddler. Say, "Look Colin. Here's a cow." Tell him the sound it makes. Say, "A cow says *moo, moo*." Ask him to imitate you and make the animal sound too.

Continue to show your toddler different animals one at a time. Encourage him to name the animal and the sound it makes. If he has trouble saying the animal's name, stretch the word out (c-o-o-w) and praise him for any sounds or true words you hear.

Do You Hear That?

Your toddler will enjoy listening to the sounds that objects make and playing with them.

Playing the Activity: Place your toddler on the floor sitting next to you. Gather some objects or toys that make stimulating sounds and place them in front of her. Pick up an object and say, "Jasmine, here is a horn. A horn goes *toot, toot*. The horn is making a *tooting* sound. Do you hear the horn going *toot toot*?" Play the horn many times for your toddler to hear. Encourage her to imitate the sounds of the

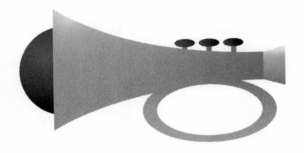

object. If you only hear her say *toot*, expand on it and say, "*Toot toot*. My horn is *tooting*."

Continue playing this game with other objects such as a bell that goes *ding, ding*, a toy car that goes *beep, beep*, or a phone that goes *ring, ring*. Praise your toddler for any sounds or words you hear her say.

Pretend Play

Your toddler will love to play and talk inside pretend spaces.

Playing the Activity: Set up a small enclosed spot for your toddler to play in. You can simply put a blanket over a large box, a toddler table, or two chairs sitting back to back. Give your toddler a few items to use in the hide out spot and talk with him while setting up. You can place a few books and toys in the hide out spot and pretend it is a school.

Next, have a conversation using simple phrases with your toddler about being in a school. Feel free to change the hide out spot to a grocery store, park, or fire station using a few related props. Finally, continue talking with your toddler using words, phrases, and simple sentences. Give him positive praise for a job well done!

Photo Pictures

Your toddler will enjoy looking at photos of friends and family and learning their names.

Playing the Activity: Place your toddler next to you as you look and point to family photographs. Say, "Look Penelope. Here's Mommy. There you are. Do you see Ralphy our dog?" As you sit with your toddler, point to each picture as you name the person or pet. Once she is familiar with the names and photos of family members and pets, ask her to point to Daddy, Mommy, Grandma, or even herself. Praise your toddler for good work and encourage her to say "Mommy" and "Daddy." You can also prompt her to say the names of other friends and family members too.

In and Out

Toddlers love to manipulate objects such as colored bears and place them in matching cups.

Playing the Activity: Place or sit your toddler at a table or on the floor sitting across from you. Gather a handful of colored bears and matching colored cups and put them in front of both of you. Drop a few red bears in a red cup and say, "Mathew, here are some red bears. Can you say bear?" Give him a red bear and have him place it in the red cup. Ask, "Can you say bear in?" If he says "bear" or "bear in," repeat the word or words a few times.

Next, ask him to dump the red bears out of the red cup and say "out" or "bears out." Continue to put the bears in and out of the matching cups.

Remind your toddler to say "in, out, bear in," and "bear out" while you play the game. Praise him for any sounds, word approximations, or true words heard.

Teapot Time

Toddlers love musical sing-a-longs. They especially love music that includes hand and body movements.

<u>Playing the Activity:</u> Tell your toddler that you are going to sing and move to "I'm a Little Teapot." Play the music on a CD player or just simply sing it. Before you start, find a toy teapot for your toddler to see and describe how the handle and spout work. Say, "Lily, you're going to act like a teapot." Begin by playing the CD or singing the song while slowly guiding her through the motions.

Encourage her to say simple words like "up, over," and "out" during your sing-a-long. You can play the song again and soon your toddler will be singing along too.

Lyrics:
> *I'm a little teapot short and stout.*
> *Here is my handle* (put hands on hips), *here is my*
> *spout* (put other arm out).
> *When I get all steamed up then I shout,*
> *Just tip me over* (lean over) *and pour me out.*

Catch the Ball

Your toddler will enjoy playing with a ball. You can teach him about turn taking as you both throw and catch the ball.

Playing the Activity: Stand across from your toddler. Hold a ball and say, "Caleb. Look, a ball." Prompt him to say "ball." Help him stretch out his arms and hands. Throw the ball gently to him. If he catches the ball, say, "Caleb, you caught the ball." If he drops it, watch it bounce and say, "Bounce, bounce. The ball is bouncing." Prompt him to say "bounce" or "ball bounce." Praise him for any sounds, word approximations, or true words you hear.

Continue throwing the ball back and forth to each other. Use words like *up*, *down*, *over*, *under*, *ball bounce*, and *catch* when playing the game. Give your toddler a little time to repeat your simple words as you play catch with the ball. Praise your toddler for good talking.

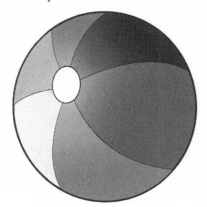

Mommy Says

Your toddler is now beginning to follow simple directions. Have her help you during your busy day or play "Mommy Says" just for fun with your toddler.

<u>Playing the Activity</u>: Stand with your toddler in the center of a room. Tell your toddler that she has to do whatever Mommy says. As you stretch out your arms say, "Elle, give Mommy a big hug." If she doesn't, say, "Mommy is giving you a big hug." Give her positive praise.

Next, point to a baby doll and say, "Bring me the baby doll." If she needs help, repeat the direction, point to the baby doll, and walk towards it with her. Encourage her to say "baby" or "my baby." If you hear sounds like "baba" or true words, expand on your toddler's utterance and say, "It is a baby. This is your baby." Praise her for doing a good job.

Have fun playing "Mommy Says" and giving one step directions with gestures such as *come here, sit down, point to the baby,* and *give me the baby.*

Smile and Say Cheese

Toddlers love to have their photographs taken during daily routines. They also enjoy looking at the photos and talking about them too.

<u>Playing the Activity:</u> Place some photographs in a pile for you and your toddler to look at together. While looking at the pictures, talk about what your toddler is doing during her daily routines.

Next, place the photos on different pages of a scrapbook. You may have a scrapbook page that shows photos of your toddler participating in story time, playtime, dress time, or mealtime. Throughout the week, show your toddler the pictures in the scrapbook that relate to whatever daily activity she is involved in. Talk about it together.

Encourage your toddler to say a few simple words about what she is doing in the photos during her daily routines. Praise her for good work.

Surprise Bag

Toddlers love surprises. You can teach your toddler to use one and two word phrases while he pulls toys out of a surprise bag.

Playing the Activity: Place your toddler on the floor beside you. Put some simple toys in a small bag (e.g., ball, train, duck, car, and bear). Show your toddler the bag and say, "Marcus, look at my surprise toy bag. Do you want to see my toys?" Say, "Open the bag. Pick something out." After he pulls out a toy, ask questions like "What is it?" or "What do you have?" If he names the toy, say, "Yes, you have a duck. You have a little duck. The duck is yellow. Push the duck." If you hear any words or word approximations praise him.

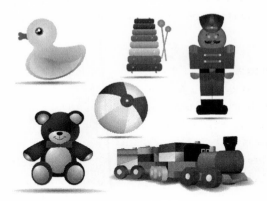

Talk about what he is doing with the toy. Ask your toddler to say "more" or "more please" when he is ready to pick more surprises out of the bag. Tell him he is doing a great job and keep on talking together about the different toys he chooses.

Flashlight Fun

A flashlight is very exciting to a young toddler. She will love shining and pointing it on different objects in the house.

<u>Playing the Activity:</u> Show your toddler how to hold and use a flashlight. Show her how it can shine on different objects in the room. Each time you shine the light on an object, name it. Say, "Look Remi. This is a door." Encourage your toddler to say "door" and talk about it with her. You can say, "The door opens and shuts." Give your toddler a chance to talk too.

Next, give your toddler the flashlight and let her shine it on an object. Ask, "What are you shining the flashlight on?" Encourage her to name the object. If she has trouble naming the object, help her with the word. Ask, "Can you say book?" Stretch out the word for her (b-o-o-k).

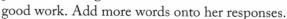

Give her positive praise for doing good work. Add more words onto her responses.

Continue to have your toddler point the flashlight on different objects in other rooms such as the kitchen, bathroom, or bedroom. Encourage her to name the objects and talk about them as you walk together around the house with a flashlight.

Time for Breakfast

Your toddler will learn lots of new words associated with breakfast when he helps you prepare the meal.

<u>Playing the Activity:</u> Walk with your toddler to the kitchen. Tell him that you need help getting breakfast ready. Say, "Jackson, we need milk. Where's the milk?" Guide him to the refrigerator and pull out the milk. Ask, "What is this?" Make sure to point to the milk. If he says "milk," praise him and repeat it. Say, "Milk. It is milk." Ask, "Do you want some milk?" Wait a few seconds for him to say "milk" or "more milk" and pour some milk in his cup. Expand on his phrases by saying, "Yes, I gave you some milk."

Repeat these steps with a spoon, bowl, cup, and cereal. Encourage your toddler to repeat one, two, and three word phrases during breakfast such as *bowl, milk, spoon, cereal, cereal please, want milk, I want milk, want more, my spoon, please, more please, all done,* and *thank you.* Praise your toddler for any word approximations or true words you hear.

Something's Missing

Your toddler will love to discover objects and toys as they appear and disappear.

Playing the Activity: Place your toddler next to you on the floor. Say, "Christie, we're going to play Something's Missing." As you begin the game, have your toddler watch you place two or three objects such as a bear, car, and ball on a tray or on the floor in a small area. Say the object's name a few times for your toddler to hear.

Tell your toddler to close and cover her eyes with her hands. Remove one of the objects and say, "Christie, something's missing!" Ask, "Do you know what's missing?" Ask her to guess or even look for the object that is missing. You can give her a clue and say, "It is furry." If she says "bear," prompt her to say "baby bear" or "furry bear" and praise her. Give your toddler a chance to remove and hide an object and have you guess or find it. Praise her for good talking!

Bear Talk

Your toddler will love talking and playing with his teddy bear as he places the bear in different locations.

Playing the Activity: Place your toddler on the floor next to you. Give him his favorite teddy bear along with a small shoebox. Tell him that teddy bear wants to go to his house. Say, "Justin, please put teddy bear in his house (shoebox). Now take teddy bear out of his house." Each time he follows a direction such as *put the teddy bear in the house*, follow by saying, "I like how you did that. You put the teddy bear in the house!"

If you hear any word approximations or true words praise him. Encourage your toddler to use two and three word phrases like "bear in, bear out," and "bear is on." Continue playing the game by placing the bear *in, out, on, off,* and *next to* different things around the house. Praise your toddler for good talking and good work.

Look and Tell

Toddlers love looking at their favorite books and talking about the pictures they see.

Playing the Activity: Place a few books in front of your toddler. Ask her to pick one favorite picture book from the pile. Sit next to her and ask questions about the pictures in the book. As you are looking at your toddler's favorite book, ask, "Serena, is that a dog? Is that a cat?" Encourage your toddler to name the animal. If she names it, expand on her response. Say, "Yes, it is a cat. A cat says meow, meow!"

If you hear one word or two word phrases, praise her. Continue to ask your toddler to name and talk about more pictures from her favorite books. Give her positive praise for good work.

Puzzles and Puzzles

Your toddler will learn new words by experimenting with puzzles. You can teach him how to take puzzles apart and put them back together.

Playing the Activity: Place your toddler next to you along with a puzzle. Say, "Willie, a puzzle!" Tell your toddler you are going to dump the puzzle out together. Say, "Look! The pieces are out." Encourage him to say "puzzle out" as he looks at the pieces on the floor. Pick up a piece of the puzzle and say, "Look, a pig." Talk to your toddler about the puzzle piece and say, "A pig says oink oink!" If you hear any word approximations or true words, praise your toddler for good talking and good work.

Next, have your toddler put a puzzle piece into an empty opening. Prompt him to say words like *put in, I put in, out,* or *I took out.* Encourage your toddler to name the puzzle piece and talk about it. Praise him for doing a terrific job. Continue taking turns while you and your toddler talk and complete the puzzle.

Sorting Fun

You can teach your toddler about sorting and identifying objects that go together.

Playing the Activity: Sit on the floor with your toddler. Place some simple objects that belong together next to your toddler such as clothes or toys. Ask your toddler to pick up an item. As she picks up a hat, say, "Look Savannah, a green hat. It's your green hat. Whose hat is it?" Prompt her to say "my hat" or "Savannah's hat." Ask your toddler to put the hat on and say, "Hat on." Praise her for following directions and tell her you like how she is using her words when she is talking.

Next, ask her to find the green mittens. As she picks them up, say, "Yes, you found the green mittens!" Tell her to put the mittens on her hands and prompt her to say "my mittens" or "Savannah's mittens." Ask questions such as "Whose hat is this?" or "Whose mittens are those?" This will allow your toddler to use words like *my* and *mine*. Continue picking up objects and talking about them with your toddler. Have fun sorting objects together.

Count with Me

Your toddler will love counting and matching items.

Playing the Activity: Sit next to your toddler at a table. Gather together some objects such as books, shoes, or blocks. Take one block and show it to your toddler. Say, "Jayden, I have one block." Encourage him to say "one block." Gesture and hold up one finger and say "one block." Next, pick up two blocks and say, "Look, two blocks." Encourage him to say "two blocks." Again, gesture and hold up two fingers and say "two blocks." Make sure you stress the /s/ sound at the end of *blocks*.

Next, pick up the books and say, "I have one book. Now I have two books." Continue playing the game with other objects such as cups, spoons, or socks. Encourage your toddler to keep on counting and praise him for a job well done!

Jump in the Puddle

Jumping and splashing through puddles after it rains is something your toddler will love doing. Talk about what you see. You might even see a rainbow in the puddle.

<u>Playing the Activity:</u> Get your toddler's raincoat, boots, and hat. Say, "Melina, we are going for a walk outside." Help her get ready and encourage her to say "boots on" or "hat on" as she puts them on. As you begin to walk outside, tell your toddler that you are looking for puddles. Say, "Look. Here's a big puddle." Prompt her to say "big" or "big puddle." As you get closer to the puddle, jump in it and say "splash" or "jump." Say, "Melina, now it's your turn. Jump! You jumped in the puddle." Again, encourage your toddler to use words like *jump, big, little, splash,* or *puddle.*

Keep on looking for big and little puddles to splash or jump into. You can even look for rainbows reflecting in the water. If you see a rainbow, name some colors and make a wish with your toddler. Have fun jumping in the puddles and keep on talking!

Blow and Pop

Toddlers love blowing things with their tiny lips. This type of movement helps strengthen the mouth muscles as your toddler learns how to talk more and more.

Playing the Activity: Sit next to your toddler. Gather together a few blowing toys such as bubble solution, wand, straw, or cotton balls. Say, "Tyler, we're going to blow some bubbles." Show your toddler how to blow bubbles with the wand. Say, "Look, Tyler. I am blowing bubbles." Encourage him to say "blowing bubbles."

Next, have him try and pop the bubbles as they float in the air. Say, "Look. I am popping bubbles. Pop. Pop." Prompt him to say "pop bubble" or "pop the bubble." Say, "Tyler, your turn to pop a bubble." Once you are done popping the floating bubbles, give the wand to your toddler. Encourage him to say "more please" or "more bubbles." Say, "Your turn to blow bubbles." Place the wand up to his lips and have him blow. Praise him for any true words or simple phrases you hear.

Let's Talk

Your toddler is beginning to use many two and three word phrases. Daily routines are an ideal time to encourage your toddler to use simple words in short phrases.

<u>Playing the Activity:</u> Share a book with your toddler during story time. Say, "Here's a book. Let's look at the pictures in the book. I see a train on the train tracks. Can you find the green train?" Help him point to the train and prompt him to say "choo-choo" or "choo-choo train." If he responds, repeat him and add more words onto his utterance. You can say, "Yes, that is a big green choo-choo train." Can you say, "Big green train?" Praise him for any words heard.

During dress time, encourage your toddler to ask for socks. Say to your toddler, "You need socks. What do you need?" If he says "socks" or "my socks," ask him to repeat you by saying, "I need socks. I want socks." Encourage him to talk

during other daily routines including mealtime, snack time, and playtime. Praise him for good talking.

Picnic Time

During playtime or snack time your toddler will enjoy having a picnic with her favorite teddy bear friends.

Playing the Activity: Place your toddler next to you on the floor. Gather two or three of your toddler's favorite teddy bear friends and a small blanket for a picnic. Place the bear friends on the blanket or on the floor in a small area along with a few cups and saucers.

Next, tell your toddler that you are going on a picnic. Hold up a cup and saucer and ask, "Anabella, what is this?" If she says "cup," say, "Yes, it is a blue cup." Then, place simple snacks in a basket and show your toddler (e.g., cookies, M&M's, goldfish crackers). Ask her what she would like to eat. Prompt her to say "cookie please" or "I want cookie." Praise her. Remind her that she is pretending to feed the teddy bear friends and needs to ask them what they want. This will allow her to ask a few "wh" questions to the bears.

During your picnic, you can read a teddy bear story and ask your toddler questions about the story. Your toddler can answer you and even ask you questions about the story. Remember to expand or add more words onto her utterances. Give your toddler positive praise for good work.

What Did You Take?

You and your toddler will have fun naming missing objects or toys and talking about them.

Playing the Activity: Sit next to your toddler. Find three common objects or toys and place them on a table or on the floor in front of your toddler (e.g., ball, bear, cup). As you point to each object ask your toddler to name it. As he is watching, take one of the objects away. Ask, "Kevin, what's missing?" If he is able to name the missing object, praise him. If he is not sure, help him by giving clues. You can say, "It is red. We drink from it." Finally, stretch out the word and say, "C-c-c-u-u-p, a red cup." Tell him, "great job" as he names the object.

You can play this game several times with many different objects. Describe the small objects using phrases and short sentences with simple words as you talk to your toddler. Say, "The car is blue. It has wheels." Ask him to repeat you and expand on his utterances by adding more words. Praise him for good talking.

Ask, Ask, Ask

Daily routines allow your toddler to express her wants and needs.

Playing the Activity: Sit your toddler at a table. Tell her that it is snack time. Set out a plate of cookies, some drinks, and napkins. Tell her to ask for one item on the table. Ask, "India, what do you want?" If she says "cookie," prompt her to say, "Cookie please. I want cookie." Following her response, give her a cookie and continue the same dialogue with the remaining items.

Prompt your toddler to ask "wh" questions. Your toddler may ask "What is it?" or "Where cookie?" Provide good models. This will give your toddler an opportunity to ask questions during snack time. Praise your toddler for good talking. Remember to add more words onto her responses to make phrases or short sentences.

Walk and Talk

Your toddler will love telling you what he sees during a walk outside or inside of the house.

Playing the Activity: Go outside with your toddler. Tell your toddler you are going for a walk in the neighborhood. As you begin to walk, point to the things you see outside and ask your toddler questions about them.

Look up in the trees. You may find a bird and point to it. Ask, "What is that Andy?" and "Can you tell me?" Continue looking up and pointing to the bird. If he says "bird," expand on his utterance and say, "Yes, it is a little bird." Ask, "What is the little bird doing?" and "Where is the bird?" Give him time to respond. If he responds "flying," say, "Yes, the bird is flying. It is flying in the sky."

Encourage your toddler to repeat your simple sentences and expand on any words or simple phrases you hear. Praise him for good talking during your conversations. Continue pointing out interesting things you see and talk about them with your toddler.

Photo Fun

Toddlers love looking at photos of themselves and family members. Have your toddler talk about who or what she sees in the photographs.

Playing the Activity: Sit next to your toddler and show her a photo of herself. Begin by asking, "Lindsay, who is that?" If she says "me" say, "Yes, that's you. You're playing with a baby doll." Ask her questions such as "What is that?" and "What are you doing?" If she responds with a one or two word phrase, expand on her words. Ask, "Whose baby is that?" and "Where is your baby?" If she says "my baby" or "my baby bed," add more words on to her response. Say, "Yes, it is your baby. Your baby doll is in bed," or "The baby doll is sleeping in her bed."

Asking questions such as "Whose baby it is?" will help your toddler respond using words like *my, mine, his,* and *hers.* Ask your toddler to imitate you and praise her for any words or phrases you hear.

Talk and Play

You can help your toddler develop two and three word phrases simply by talking during playtime.

Playing the Activity: Sit on the floor with your toddler. Place some toys on the floor such as balls, bears, cars, or blocks. Pick up a few cars and say, "Sean, I like *cars*." Next pick up a few balls and say, "I like *balls*."

Then, pick up a few bears and say, "I like _____," and let your toddler fill in the blank. If he has difficulty, prompt him to fill in the blank and have him repeat the phrase back to you. Finally, ask your toddler what he likes as he is playing with the toys. Repeat any words you hear from your toddler and add new words onto his utterances.

Continue playing this game with different toys and objects. Encourage your toddler to use words or simple phrases and praise him for good talking.

Shopping for Food

Your toddler will love to explore the isles of the grocery store. There is so much to see and so much to talk about.

Playing the Activity: Walk or drive with your toddler to the grocery store. Tell your toddler that you are taking her shopping for food. On your way, discuss what you need to buy. Say, "Naomi, I need apples, bread, and milk from the grocery store. Can you help me find them at the store?" Once you get there, pick out your items.

Help your toddler name the food items and help her describe each one. Say, "Naomi, here are the apples. Can you say apple?" If she says "apple" say, "Yes, it is an apple. It is a big red apple. What is it?" If she says "a red apple," praise her. Model simple sentences and praise your toddler for any words or phrases heard.

Match It

Matching objects and pictures will help increase your toddler's vocabulary words. You can use your toddler's favorite figurines or toy objects that he plays with everyday.

Playing the Activity: Sit with your toddler at a table or on the floor. Find an old toy box that has pictures of your toddler's favorite characters or toy objects on it. Cut the pictures out of the box. Gather the figurines or toy objects that go along with the box. Say, "Joey, look. We are going to play a matching game."

Place four or five pictures of the figurines in front of your toddler. Hand him a figurine and say, "Look, this is Bubbles the fish. Can you find his picture?" If he points to it, ask, "Can you put Bubbles on his picture? If he does, say, "You found Bubbles the fish. Bubbles' is yellow. He lives in the water."

Encourage your toddler to say a few words about the figurine that he matches. Provide good verbal models and continue having him match up the objects with pictures. Praise him and keep on talking using phrases or simple sentences when communicating with your toddler.

Washing Up

Getting ready for the day is a great time to talk to your toddler. Your toddler will learn the names of objects and learn to talk using simple sentences while washing up.

Playing the Activity: Walk with your toddler to the bathroom. Tell your toddler that it is time to get washed up. Have a few objects ready such as soap and a washcloth. Say, "Marisa, it's time to wash your face. Can you tell me what we need?" If she says "soap," prompt her to say, "I need soap" or "I want the soap." Ask, "What else do you need?" If she says "a washcloth," prompt her to say, "I want a washcloth. I need a washcloth." Not only is she naming objects but she is also making simple sentences.

You can also talk with your toddler about brushing her teeth and combing her hair. Encourage her to use words like *washing, dressing, combing,* and *brushing* as she talks to you about starting her busy day. Praise her for good work.

Take a Ride

Your toddler will love going for a ride in the car. Along the way you can strike up a conversation about anything you see.

Playing the Activity: Place your toddler in a car seat in your vehicle. Tell him that you are going for a long ride in the neighborhood. While riding in the car with your toddler, look for familiar things that you both can talk about. For example, your toddler may see a bus. If he says "a bus," add more words to make a phrase or simple sentence. Say, "Yes, Isaiah, that is a big yellow bus. I see the big bus too. Can you say big yellow bus?" Expand on his simple utterance by adding more words. Praise him for good talking.

You can point out and talk about familiar people, vehicles, or animals during the ride in the car with your toddler. Continue to talk by modeling phrases and simple sentences. Praise your toddler for good work.

Go Fish

Your toddler will enjoy fishing for sea creatures as she learns about spatial concepts including *in* and *out*. Your toddler will also enjoy wiggling like a fish and splashing like a dolphin.

Playing the Activity: Place your toddler next to you on a plastic mat or blanket outside in the backyard. Gather together some colorful toy sea animals and a fishing pole or fishing net. Say, "Alanah, we're going fishing." Fill a bowl with some water and place it on the mat.

Next, ask, "Alanah, can you put some sea animals in the water?" Make sure to stress the phrase "in the water." Praise her for doing a good job. Give her the fishing pole and ask, "Can you get two fish out of the water?" As she starts fishing, say, "Alanah, you are catching some fish. You are getting the fish out of the water." Again, stress the phrase "out of the water." While she is fishing, ask, "Where are the fish?" If she responds "in the water," praise her. If she needs help, repeat and model the simple phrase for her. Add more words onto her phrases to make short sentences. Have fun getting the fish in and out of the water.

Moving Like an Animal

Your toddler will enjoy talking about different kinds of animals with you and moving like them too!

Playing the Activity: Stand next to your toddler. Tell him to watch you as you move like an animal. Begin by hopping like a rabbit in place and say, "I am a rabbit Sammy. What am I doing?" If he says "hopping," say, "Yes, I am hopping like a rabbit. Can you do it?" As your toddler begins to hop, ask, "What animal are you?" If he says "rabbit," prompt him to say, "I am a rabbit. I like to hop."

Next, ask your toddler, "What are you doing?" If he says "jumping," prompt him to say, "I am jumping." Ask your toddler, "What animal are you now?" He may say, "a frog" or "a dog." Remember to expand on his responses and help your toddler make simple sentences as you interact with him.

Continue playing the game with your toddler by imitating different animal movements and asking simple questions. Be sure to give him a little time to think about what he wants to say. There are so many animals to imitate, so have fun moving like an animal with your toddler. Praise him for using words, phrases, or simple sentences.

Mealtime Fun

Your toddler is talking so much more now. She may be using two, three, and four word phrases. Mealtime is the perfect time for your toddler to ask for something she may want using phrases or simple sentences.

<u>Playing the Activity:</u> Sit next to your toddler at a table. If it is breakfast time, you can place simple objects and food out such as a bowl, spoon, juice, milk, and cereal. Tell your toddler it is time to eat breakfast.

Next, ask, "Sabrina, what do you want?" If she says "bowl" prompt her to say, "I want a bowl. Give me a bowl. Can I have a bowl?" Ask her to repeat your simple sentences or questions back to you and say,  "Sabrina, what else do you want?" If she says "cereal," prompt her to say, "I want cereal. Can I have cereal?" Praise her for good talking and give her the items she requested.

Continue to have her ask for the remaining breakfast items. Your toddler will enjoy talking to you during mealtime and this is the perfect time for you to expand and add more words onto your toddler's phrases or simple sentences.

Is It Big or Little?

You can help your toddler learn about objects that are big and little by comparing objects around the house.

Playing the Activity: Walk around the house with your toddler. As you walk, gather up simple objects such as spoons, keys, cups, plates, or shoes. Tell your toddler that you are going to place the big objects in one pile and the little objects in another pile. Pick up an object and say, "Benjamin, I have a big boot. Now I have a big doll." Place the big items next to each other in the big pile. Ask, "Can you find something big?" If he picks up a big object, ask, "What it is?" If he says "a cup," say, "Yes, that is a big green cup. We drink from a cup." Have your toddler repeat your simple sentences back to you.

Continue sorting the items in two piles (e.g., big and little). Once you finish sorting by size, you can ask your toddler to give you items from each pile. Say, "Benjamin, give me a big spoon and a little key." Continue playing the game together and provide your toddler with positive praise.

Memory Game

Toddlers love to play memory games with different objects.

Playing the Activity: Place some objects on a tray. Take a few minutes to talk to your toddler about what is on the tray. Say, "Leila, I see a crayon." Ask, "What do you do with a crayon?" If she says "Color paper," say, "Yes, you do color paper with a crayon." Prompt her to say, "I am coloring paper" or "I am coloring with my crayon."

Next, find another item on the tray. Say, "Look. Here is a ball. You bounce a ball. What do you do with a ball?" If she says "Bounce a ball," praise her and say, "Yes, you can bounce the ball!" Now, ask your toddler to cover her eyes as you take an item off the tray and hide it. Say, "Open your eyes. Something is missing? Do you know what it is?" If she is not sure, give her a clue and say, "You drink from it." If she responds "cup," say, "Yes, Leila, it is a small yellow cup. Can you say that?" Ask her to repeat your simple sentences back to you.

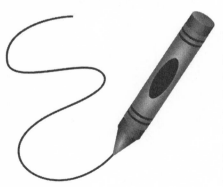

Continue playing the game by hiding more of the objects. Repeat and add more words onto your toddler's responses as she tells you what is missing. Praise her for good talking.

Counting, Matching, and Stacking

This game will help your toddler learn how to count, match, and stack colored blocks.

Playing the Activity: Sit next to your toddler at a table. Gather together some colored blocks (e.g., red, green, blue, yellow). Say, "Keyon, let's make a blue tower." Pick up a blue block and say, "I have a blue block." Show your toddler the blue block. Ask, "Can you find me a blue block?" As he finds a blue block, ask, "What is that?" If he says "blue block," say, "Yes, you found a blue block. You have one blue block."

Begin to stack the blocks and have your toddler stack them too. While you are stacking the blocks say, "One blue block, two blue blocks, and three blue blocks." Encourage your toddler to count with you. Make sure he adds the "*s*" on the end of the word *blocks*. Continue making a red, green, and yellow tower with the remaining blocks.

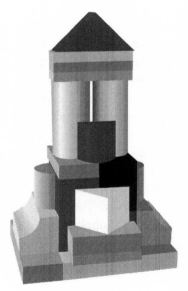

Shopping at Home

Your toddler will enjoy a pretend shopping trip in your home with you.

Playing the Activity: Sit next to your toddler at a table. Place some toy food items on a table for your toddler to see. Say, "Karissa, we need to buy some food from the food store. Here is a bag for you. Let's go shopping! What would you like to buy?" If she responds using only one or two words, repeat and add more words onto her phrases. If she says "milk," prompt her to say, "I want some milk. Can I have milk?" Praise her and continue shopping.

Encourage your toddler to talk about what she is buying from her pretend food store. Prompt her to ask you "wh" questions about *what* she wants and *where* it is. Expand and add more words onto her phrases and simple sentences as she enjoys her little shopping trip.

I See Something

Toddlers love to spy things with their little eyes.

Playing the Activity: Place or sit with your toddler on the floor. Tell your toddler that you are going to play a game called "I See Something." Gather a few simple objects or toys such as sunglasses, pail, shovel, drinking cups, teddy bear, hair brush, and toy car.

Next, place four objects in front of your toddler. Say, "I'm going to tell you something about one of these objects. You have to guess what I am thinking of. Take a good look at the objects." Give your first clue by saying, "Nathan, I see something that you wear on your eyes. Can you guess what it is?" If he says "sunglasses," praise him. Encourage him to tell you something about *sunglasses* using a simple sentence. Prompt him to say something like "I wear shiny sunglasses. My sunglasses are green."

Continue playing "I See Something." Prompt your toddler to repeat your simple sentences and encourage him to keep on talking about what he sees. Give him verbal praise for a job well done.

Color Time

Your toddler will love matching and sorting colored objects.

Playing the Activity: Sit on the floor with your toddler. Gather different colored teddy bears and cups. Place them in front of your toddler. Tell her you are going to match the teddy bears together by color. Help her sort the bears. Say, "Jane, here is a blue bear. Here's another blue bear. Can you find a blue bear?" If she grabs a blue bear, say, "You found a blue bear. You are doing a great job!" Encourage your toddler to say, "Little blue bear" or "I have a little blue bear." Give her positive praise for using her words.

Help your toddler place the remaining blue bears into the blue cup. Be sure to encourage your toddler to talk about matching the teddy bears with the cups. Expand and add more words onto your toddler's responses as you help her match and sort the colored objects. Praise your toddler for good talking.

Let's Make a Book

Your toddler will love cutting and pasting pictures of things he likes and creating a book of his own.

<u>Playing the Activity:</u> Sit next to your toddler. Ask your toddler to tell you what he sees as he flips through a magazine. If your toddler points to a dog, talk about what it is and what the dog is doing. You can then cut it out and start a category pile. Place the picture of the dog into the animal pile along with other animals that you find with your toddler. Continue looking for items that belong in categories such as toys, colored shapes, cartoon characters, community helpers, vehicles, food, and clothes.

Once you have found enough pictures to cut out, have your toddler help you paste them onto paper. Try to keep the pictures together by category. This will allow your toddler to understand which items belong together. Leave enough space on each page for him to write true words above or below the pictures as he gets older. Now you and your toddler have created a book that you both can enjoy together.

Encourage your toddler to talk about his book and his favorite pictures. Remember to ask him questions such as "What is it?" and "What does it look like?" You can also ask, "Where do you find it?" or "Where does he work?" Prompt your toddler to ask you "wh" questions about his favorite pictures in his book. Provide good models. Praise your toddler for using phrases or simple sentences and expand on his responses.

Reading Time

Reading stories to your toddler will help stimulate your toddler's language skills and allow her to learn so many new words.

Playing the Activity: Sit next to your toddler. Gather a few books for you and your toddler to read. Ask, "Bella, can you pick out a book?" The books should have simple pictures with short sentences. While you are reading, make sure to point to the pictures and words so she can follow along.

Encourage your toddler to talk about what she sees as you look at the pictures in the story together. Ask her simple questions as you read the story such as "Where is the girl?" and "What is the girl doing?" If she answers with only one or two words, help her by adding more words onto her responses to make simple sentences. You can always retell the story to your toddler and soon she will be repeating it back to you. Praise her for good work.

Furry Friends

You can help your toddler learn the names of many furry creatures by looking at picture books of animals and asking simple questions about them.

Playing the Activity: Sit next to your toddler at a table. Gather some picture books of farm and zoo animals for you and your toddler to look at together. As you look at the zoo picture book, say, "Look Jeffrey, a bear. The bear has brown fur (touch the brown fur). The bear has four paws (count the paws). Can you find and point to the bear?" As he points to the bear, ask, "What color is the bear?" and "Where is the bear?" You can also ask, "Is the bear little or big?" and "How many paws does the bear have?"

Encourage your toddler to use simple sentences when responding to your questions. He may say, "The bear is big. The bear is furry." Give him a few seconds to respond to your questions. Praise him for good talking and terrific work. Keep on asking your toddler questions and talking together as you pick out more furry friends from the picture books.

My Fun Box

A box with your toddler's favorite treasures will allow you and your toddler to talk about memories from the past.

Playing the Activity: Look for an empty box. Help your toddler decorate it with her favorite colored paper or stickers. Tell your toddler that you are going to find some fun toys, photographs, and special objects (e.g., seashell, rabbit's foot, ball, sand dollar, stickers, keychain) from her room.

As you start collecting objects, talk about what each item is and the memory it brings. Ask, "What is this, Jules?" Give her a moment to respond. If she says "rabbit's foot," say, "Yes, it's a white rabbit's foot." Talk about what a rabbit's foot is and how it feels. Then ask, "Jules, do you remember where you got this from?" Give her clues if she has difficulty remembering. You can say, "Giraffes, monkeys, and elephants live in the _____?" If she says "the zoo," expand on her response and say, "The rabbit's foot is from the zoo!" Have fun talking about your toddler's favorite treasures and putting them in her fun box.

Games for Preschoolers

Nursery Rhyme Time

Your child will enjoy singing and listening to fingerplay songs or nursery rhymes such as "The Wheels on the Bus" or "Twinkle Twinkle Little Star."

<u>Playing the Activity:</u> Stand face to face with your child. Sing a nursery rhyme or fingerplay song. As you sing, move your hands in motion and leave off a word or two in each line. Say, "The wheels on the bus go round and _____. The horn on the bus goes beep, _____, _____." As you continue singing the song, leave off more and more words. You can sing other songs and leave off a few of the words like "Twinkle twinkle little _____, how I wonder what you _____." Eventually your child will be singing the complete song back to you.

What Color Did You Eat?

You and your child can talk about foods and their colors. This will help your child identify the colors of her favorite foods.

Playing the Activity: Sit with your child at a table. Ask your child to think about what she ate for lunch or dinner. Say, "Geena, we had spaghetti and meatballs for dinner. My spaghetti was red. What color was your spaghetti?" If she says "red" or "it was red," say, "Yes, your spaghetti was red. Did you eat anything else red?" Give her a clue. If she responds correctly praise her. If she needs help, ask, "What about the round little balls in the green leafy salad?" If she says "tomatoes," say, "Yes, the tomatoes are red and round." If she is unable to remember, continue giving her clues such as "They are red, round, and juicy." Praise her for good talking.

Continue asking about colors of foods your child ate during other meals of the day. Help your child to form sentences using descriptive words as she answers your questions.

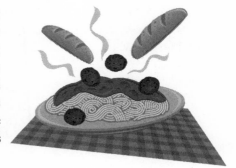

Describe It

Your child's vocabulary is exploding with new words every day. You will also notice that your child's sentences are becoming longer too. Describing objects or toys will help your child to think, enhance vocabulary and memory skills, and increase his sentence length.

Playing the Activity: Sit at a table with your child. Write down some simple words (e.g., dog, cat, ball, drum, car) on small cards or paper and place them in a paper bag. Help your child pick one out. Read the word to him. Say, "Derrick, it says dog. Can you think of any words that describe a dog?" You can give him verbal cues by asking questions such as "How does it feel?" or "Is it big or little?"

Help your child think of at least four words to describe the word "dog." Use descriptive words like *furry*, *soft*, *big*, *little*, *brown*, *white*, and *black*. Ask him to use a few of the words in a sentence like "The dog is furry and soft." Help your child describe the remaining words in the paper bag using simple sentences. Remember to give your child positive praise for good work.

Does It Belong?

Your child will enjoy talking about objects that belong together.

Playing the Activity: Find a few objects in your house that belong with other objects (e.g., comb, remote control, spoon, toothbrush, brush). Ask your child what goes with a toothbrush. As your child begins to answer, prompt her to think of more words related to a toothbrush. If she says "teeth" or "toothpaste," model a few sentences using the new words. You can say, "I brush my teeth with a toothbrush. I put toothpaste on my toothbrush." Ask her to repeat the sentences back to you. Praise her for good talking.

Encourage your child to talk about more objects and why they belong together. You can even have your child ask you questions about the objects that belong together.

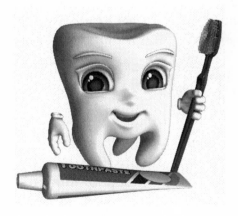

Game of Opposites

Your child will enjoy learning and acting out words that are opposite pairs.

Playing the Activity: Sit at a table with your child. Write down opposite pairs on the front and back of small cards or paper (e.g., up/down, in/out, girl/boy, hot/cold, fast/slow, yes/no, big/little). Place the cards in a bag and have your child pick one. Help your child sound out the word and say the word a few times. Next, ask, "Richie what is the word?" If he says "up," ask, "Can you put your arms up?" As he begins to raise his arms up, ask, "What are you doing Richie?" Prompt him to say, "I am putting my arms up in the air." If he has trouble, model a shorter sentence with simple words and have him repeat it back to you.

After your child responds, continue playing the game of opposites. Ask, "Do you know what the opposite of *up* is?" If he knows, praise him. If he doesn't, look at the back of the card. Say, "It says down. My arms are up and now they are _____." Ask your child to imitate your arm movements and say, "Up, down, up, and down."

Continue to act out the opposite pairs as you talk about them. Also, expand and add words onto to your child's responses to form simple sentences. Give your child verbal praise for doing a great job.

Can You Say It?

Your child will enjoy answering questions about what she sees as you walk together outside. She will also like making sentences and repeating them back to you.

Playing the Activity: Go outside with your child. Start pointing out things you see as you are walking. You can say to your child, "I see some flowers." As the two of you look at the flowers, begin to ask your child questions. Ask, "Hailey, what color are the flowers?" If she says "pink," say, "Yes, the flowers are pink. The flowers have pink petals. Where are the flowers?" If she says "in the garden," say, "Yes, the pink flowers are in the garden. Can you say that?"

Continue to ask more questions and add more descriptive words onto your child's responses to help her build longer sentences using related vocabulary words. Ask your child to repeat the sentences back to you. As you continue walking, prompt your child to ask you "wh" (what, where, why) questions about what you see outside. Praise your child for good talking.

Follow the Directions

Your child will use his memory skills to carry out complex commands with two and three actions.

Playing the Activity: Stand face to face with your child. Say, "Scotty, I want you to listen carefully to everything I say. I want you to wiggle your body and jump in place." If he follows the directions, say, "Good job. Now I want you to cover your eyes and touch your head."

Once he shows that he understands two step commands, add a third command. You can say, "Scotty, clap your hands, touch your nose, and wiggle your body." Continue to give your child two and three step directions to follow. Praise him for good listening as he completes them.

Listen Up

Your child can learn to strengthen her listening skills by playing listening games.

Playing the Activity: Walk around the house with your child. Next, have your child listen for sounds over and over again within your home (e.g., doorbell ringing, knocking on the door, clapping hands, stomping feet on the floor, running water, splashing water, closing the door, crumpling paper). Once your child has a chance to listen to sounds in the home, begin the game. Help your child cover her eyes as you give clues and ask her if she knows what is making the sound. If she guesses correctly, continue walking around the house to identify more and more sounds.

You can have your child talk in sentences by providing good models as she identifies the sounds she hears. She may say, "I hear bells ringing. The door is closing." Add more words onto her sentences. Praise her for good talking and good work. Continue playing the game and listening for different sounds around the house.

In the Box

Talking about how things feel will help your child think of the right words to describe them.

Playing the Activity: Walk around the house with your child. As you walk, have your child help you gather together some small toys or household items such as sunglasses, ball, teddy bear, marbles, blocks, cotton balls, pen, keys, cups, and spoons.

Next, place the items in a box. Ask your child to pick one item out of the box with his eyes closed. Help him touch the item and describe it.

Ask, "Noah, how does it feel?" Give him verbal cues if he needs help.

You can ask, "Is it rough like sandpaper or smooth like shiny sunglasses? Do you know?" If he answers with only a few words, expand on his response. As your child describes the items in the box, help him use descriptive words like *bumpy, hard, soft, round, smooth, small, little,* and *big*.

Encourage him to use complete sentences as he talks about the items that he picks out of the box. Continue playing the game and praise your child for using descriptive words.

Story Telling

Looking at picture books allows your child to tell her own story and increase her vocabulary skills.

Playing the Activity: Sit at a table with your child. Place a picture book in front of her. Tell her that she is going to be a storyteller by describing what she sees in the picture book. As your child describes the pictures, ask her related questions. Your child may say, "I see a girl." Ask, "Destiny, what is the girl doing?" If she says "making a snowman," ask, "What does the snowman look like?" Prompt her to use some descriptive words to describe the snowman like *white, round, little, big, tall, short, happy,* or *sad.*

Next, help your child put her two responses together to make one sentence and say, "I see a girl making a snowman. She is making a big snowman." Continue asking questions such as "How do you make a snowman?" or "Can you describe the snowman's face?" She may say, "He has black eyes. His nose is orange." If she responds with only a few words expand on her response and say, "The snowman has black eyes and an orange nose." Ask her to repeat the sentence back to you and give her verbal praise.

Again, encourage your child to put two responses together to make one sentence. Continue having her tell a story that is related to the pictures in the book. Expand on your child's responses or simple sentences by adding more words and providing verbal models when needed.

Plant a Garden

Planting a garden will help your child learn about different kinds of vegetables and allow him to follow step-by-step directions.

Playing the Activity: Talk about the steps needed to plant a garden with your child. Gather together some garden tools. Show a tool to your child and ask, "Martin, do you know what tool this is?" If he responds "shovel," say, "Yes, it's a shovel. We dig in the garden with a shovel." Ask him to repeat the sentence back to you and provide verbal cues if necessary. Show him more tools (e.g., hoe, rake, watering can) and help him build simple sentences as he talks about the tools. Remind him that he will need to dig up the soil with the garden tools.

Next, tell your child that it is time to decide what vegetable seeds to plant in the soil. Ask, "Martin, can you name some vegetables that grow in a garden?" Prompt your child to name vegetables including *lettuce*, *tomatoes*, *cucumbers*, *broccoli*, *carrots*, *green beans*, *corn*, and *onions*. If he needs help, give him verbal cues using descriptive words such as *leafy*, *skinny*, *round*, *flowery*, *pointy*, *orange*, and *long*.

Finally, ask your child to tell you what we need to do last when planting a garden. If he says "water the garden," praise him and expand on his sentence. Say, "We water the garden with a watering can." If he is unsure about the last step, show him the watering can and talk about it with him. Ask your child to repeat the steps involved in planting a garden.

Prompt your child to talk about planting a garden using longer sentences with proper garden vocabulary. If he responds using a few words, make sure to expand and add more words onto his responses and have him repeat them back to you. Now he is ready to plant a garden.

Fun in the Sun

Summertime is a great time to walk on the beach with your child and talk about what you can see, touch, hear, and taste. This is a great activity to help increase your child's memory skills.

Playing the Activity: Pack your car for a trip to the beach. Tell your child to put on her swimsuit and grab her beach towel. When you and your child arrive take some time to talk about what you both see and then begin to ask her questions. Ask, "Brielle, can you tell me what you see at the beach?"

As your child starts naming things she sees at the beach have her close her eyes. See if she can remember things she saw and also name things she may have not seen. Give her clues if necessary. Say, "Brielle, I'm thinking of a slimy plant. You find it in the water. Can you tell me?" If she says "seaweed," say, "Yes, it is seaweed." If she has difficulty, give her verbal prompts and cues to help her think of the word. Help her make a sentence using the words *seaweed*, *plant*, and *water* and have her repeat the sentence back to you.

Continue the game by having your child name things she can see, hear, touch, and taste at the beach. Help her think of words like *blanket*, *lifeguard*, *chair*, *suntan lotion*, *sunglasses, sand, seashell, ocean, fish, starfish, seahorse, waves, food* and more. You can have her build longer sentences using words she recalls. Remember to give her time to think and respond as she keeps on playing "Fun in the Sun" with you. Praise her for good talking.

What Did You Say?

Understanding, listening, and recalling information are important language skills that your child will need to acquire.

Playing the Activity: Sit next to your child. Tell him that you are going to play a listen and tell game. Say a sentence that has important information for your child to remember. You can say, "Today is Friday and it is sunny. Ezra, what day is it?" If he says "Friday," say, "Yes, it's Friday!" If this is easy for him, ask him to listen again. Say, "It is 10 o'clock on Friday and 65 degrees outside." Now ask, "What day is it and what time is it?" If he answers correctly, praise him and ask, "Can you also tell me the temperature outside?" Praise him if he is able to recall the correct information. If he has difficulty recalling the details, reduce the amount of information in your sentences and provide verbal cues. Praise him for good talking.

Continue asking questions with information such as *birthday, age, address, phone number, city,* and *state.* You might say, "Ezra, your birthday is May 17th and you are four years old. When is your birthday and how old are you?" If he needs verbal prompts, provide them and praise him. You can also say to your child, "You live on 75 Washington Street in White Plains, New York. Now, can you tell me what street you live on, along with the city and state?"

You can modify or make your statements and questions more difficult depending on how well your child responds to them. Give verbal prompts or cues if your child has difficulty recalling specific information. Praise your child for good work.

Let's Pretend

Pretend role playing can help your child develop topic sentences and conversation skills.

Playing the Activity: Sit next to your child. Help your child pick out two of her favorite puppets or stuffed animals. Say, "Autumn, teddy bear needs to get ready for school. What should he do?" If she says "wash his face," ask, "What else should the teddy bear do?" Again, your child may say "brush his teeth." Say, "Good. Is there something else he should do?" If she says "comb his hair," say, "Very good."

Now have your child put a few of her responses together to make one sentence. You can model a sentence for her and say, "Teddy bear needs to wash his face and brush his teeth." Ask your child to repeat your sentence back to you. If it is too difficult for her, reduce the length of the sentence. Say, "Teddy bear needs to wash his face." As your child is talking, make sure she stays on topic. Provide verbal prompts and cues as needed.

Continue talking with your child and role playing with her puppets or stuffed animals.

Hunting for Colors

Help your child learn colors by searching for them in and out of the house.

Playing the Activity: Sit at a table with your child. You will need to cut three red circles, three green triangles, and three blue squares out of colored paper. Tell your child that you are going on a color hunt in and out of your house. You can have your child carry a paper bag during the hunt. Show your child the colored shapes and say, "Ryan, pick a color." Ask your child, "What colored shape did you pick?" He may say, "I picked green." Ask, "What letter does green begin with?" If he says "g," praise him. If he has difficulty

recalling the letter "g," prompt him by making the sound "ga, ga, ga." Say, "Green begins with the letter "g."

Next, give your child the three green triangles and say, "Let's go hunting for colors." Prompt your child to look for green things on tables, on pictures, on walls, or in closets. Ask, "Ryan, did you find something green?" Your child may respond, "I found a green shirt." Ask, "Where did you find the green shirt?" If your child says "in the closet," add more words onto his response. Ask your child to repeat the complete sentence back to you. Praise him and write down *shirt* on the back of the green triangle and place it in the bag. Continue hunting for colors. After you are done looking inside, go outside with your child.

Tell him that you have two more green triangles. Give your child clues and say, "Look on the porch, in the tree, or in the garden. Just keep looking." Again, ask, "Ryan, can you find something green out here?" If he says "A green leaf," say, "Good job." Then, ask, "What letter does leaf begin with?" If he says "l," praise him. If he needs a verbal cue, say, "la, la, la," and name the letter if he has trouble. Name other words that begin with the letter "l."

Continue asking questions during the game such as "Where is the green leaf?" If your child responds correctly, praise him. If he needs help, expand on his sentence or model it for him. Say, "The green leaf is hanging on the tall tree." Ask him to repeat the sentence back to you and give him verbal praise. Again, write down the word *leaf* on the back of the green triangle and have him place it in the bag.

Once you are done finding green things, you can switch to a new color. If your child needs a challenge, have him search for items that are purple, orange, or yellow. At the end of the game, have your child take the colored shapes out of the bag. Help him read the words on the back of the shapes. Encourage him to describe the colored items that he found in and out of the house using sentences. Praise him for doing great work.

Searching for Shapes

Help your child learn about different shapes by searching for them around the house.

Playing the Activity: Sit at a table with your child. Draw a circle, square, triangle, and rectangle at the top of a piece of paper. Write the word circle, square, triangle, and rectangle under each shape. Talk about the shapes and their differences. Next, tell your child you are going to look for different shapes around the house. Say, "Myli, let's go to your bedroom and find some shapes." Bring your paper and mark an (X) under the shapes you find. Ask, "Do you see anything shaped like a rectangle or square in your room?" If she says "my bed," ask, "What shape do you think it is?" Show her the paper and point to the shapes if she needs help. If she says "that one," say, "Good, that is a  rectangle. What shape is it, Myli?" If she says "rectangle," say, "Yes, your bed is shaped like a rectangle. Can you say that?" If she has trouble, help her by giving verbal cues and praise her for repeating the sentence back to you.

Next, have her put a mark (X) under the rectangle on the paper chart. Ask, "Do you see anymore shapes in this room?" She may say "a circle." Prompt her to say, "I see a circle." Ask, "What is shaped like a circle?" Your child may say "my clock." Praise her. Have her mark an (X) under the circle on the paper chart. Now help your child put a few of her responses together to form complete sentences. Say, "My bed is shaped like a rectangle. My clock is shaped like a circle." Have your child repeat these sentences back to you. Provide her with verbal prompts if she needs help and praise her.

Continue searching for shapes in the house. Once you are done, ask your child if she can remember where she found the different shapes and what they were. You can ask her how many shapes she found altogether during her search. She can also count all the shapes to see which shape she has the most of and which shape she has the least of.

Finally, your child can describe her favorite shapes back to you. She may say, "A circle is round" or "A square has four sides." Give her verbal cues if she needs help making a complete sentence. Enjoy searching for shapes around the house with your child.

Do You Know?

Preschoolers love to talk about their families and people they're familiar with.

Playing the Activity: Sit at a table with your child. Tell your child you are going to talk about a family member. Say, "Henry, I want to talk about someone in our family. Can you pick someone?" Your child may say, "I pick Dad." Say, "Good. Let's talk about your Dad."

Begin by asking your child some personal questions about the family member he picks. Ask, "What does Daddy do at work?" As you ask questions, prompt your child to answer using complete sentences with descriptive vocabulary. Prompt your child to say, "Daddy is a policeman. He drives a black police car." Next, ask your child, "Where does Daddy work?" If he says "a police station,"  prompt him to say, "He works at a police station. He works in the city downtown."

Repeat and expand on your child's responses by adding more words. Prompt him to use vocabulary words such as *uniform*, *police car*, *vehicle*, *siren*, *city*, and *badge* during your conversation. You can model a few sentences for your child too and say, "Daddy wears a police uniform. He wears a badge on his uniform." Ask your child to repeat the sentences back to you. If your child says "Daddy is a banker," prompt him to use vocabulary words such as *bank, office, briefcase, desk, tall building, downtown, computer,* and *meetings.*

As you carry on your conversation you can also ask questions such as "What is Dad's favorite food?" or "What sports does he like?" How about asking, "What do you and Daddy do for fun?" Give your child time to respond to your questions and praise him for good talking.

Remember to have your child use words related to the topic when building sentences such as *basketball, football, baseball, hockey,* or *soccer.* If Dad likes basketball, help your child think of words associated with basketball and put the related words in sentences.

Once your child is done talking about Dad, have him pick someone else to talk about. Encourage your child to use longer and longer sentences when talking about family members. Give your child verbal praise for doing a great job.

So Many Words

You can help your child increase her vocabulary and make sentences by playing word games.

Playing the Activity: Think of something that your child enjoys doing such as swimming, sledding, or going for a walk outdoors. Say, "Lola, I want you to help me think of words that remind you of going to the beach." Say, "I'm going swimming at the _(blank)_ today." Ask your child to fill in the blank and begin thinking of words related to the beach. Give your child verbal cues if she needs help thinking of words.

If she says the word "water," ask her to describe what water looks like and how it feels.

As your child thinks of words, write them down for her. Once she is finished thinking of words related to the beach, tell her that she is going to make up sentences using the new words that she thought of. Refer back to her word list and say, "Lola, you came up with the words *sand* and *beach blanket*. Can you put sand and beach blanket in a sentence?" Give her verbal cues as needed. You can challenge your child by having her use three of her words together in a longer sentence.

You can also have your child ask you "wh" questions about what you might see at the beach too. This will reinforce the vocabulary words that she thought of when talking about swimming at the beach. Enjoy building complete sentences together using descriptive words. Give her verbal praise.

Put the Words Together

Your child will enjoy talking about how some words go together and how some do not. This will help your child develop good thinking and memory skills.

Playing the Activity: Sit at a table with your child. On a sheet of paper list four or five words that go together along with one word that doesn't belong (e.g., dog, cat, bird, comb, and fish). Ask your child, "Can you tell me which word does not belong in the group?" If your child says "comb," say, "Good," and ask, "Why doesn't it belong?" Give verbal prompts if needed.

Enhance your child's thinking skills by asking questions such as "How are cat and dog the same?" and "How are they different?" Help your child by talking about how the words are alike and different by using descriptive words in complete sentences.

Other categories your child can talk about include toys, food, colors, and shapes. Challenge your child by thinking of harder words that go together in categories such as musical instruments, clothing, sports, vehicles, and insects. Remember to keep on talking!

Walk in the Snow

Your child will enjoy walking outside on a snowy day. Talk about the wintry things you see using compound words such as snowman or snowball.

Playing the Activity: Walk to the closet with your child. Tell your child that he is going for a walk outside and remind him to bundle up because it's chilly. As you walk in the snow, tell your child to think of words that have the word "snow" in them. Ask, "Sonny, can you tell me what is falling from the sky?" If he says "snow," say, "Yes, there's lots of white snow falling down from the sky."

Next, tell your child to think of a word that goes with "snow." Give your child a clue by providing him with a rhyming word. Say, "Sonny, the word rhymes with cake. I'm thinking of a snow _____." You can give him visual and verbal cues such as "fl" and stretch it out (f-l-a-k-e). If he says "flake," say, "Yes. Now you can add *snow* to the word *flake* and make *snow* _____." Say, "Sonny, you made a compound word by putting two words together to make one word."

As you continue to walk in the snow, think of other wintry compound words such as *snowman, snowball, snowmobile, snowsuit, snowplow, snowshoe, snowbird, snowstorm,* and *snowdrift*. Encourage your child to use the compound words in complete sentences. If he needs help, model five to eight word sentences and have him repeat them back to you. Encourage your child to talk about what he sees as you walk together outside in the snow. Praise your child for good talking.

What's in the Ocean?

Your child can use descriptive adjectives when learning about sea animals that live in the ocean.

Playing the Activity: Sit next to your child at a table. Gather some squishy sea animal toys (e.g., shark, fish, starfish, lobster, crab, octopus). Place them on a small blue towel, blue blanket, or piece of blue construction paper in front of your child.

Next, tell your child that she is going to catch some sea animals using a fishing net or a small cup. Give her the small fishing net and ask, "Shana, what's in the ocean?" As she catches a sea animal, ask her to describe what she caught. If she says "I caught a shark," ask her questions about the shark.

Help her build sentences using descriptive words to describe what she caught in the ocean such as "I caught a nasty shark with sharp teeth." Ask her to repeat the sentences back to you and provide verbal cues if she has difficulty.

As your child continues to play the game, have her talk about each of the sea animals using sentences with descriptive vocabulary words such as *small, large, tiny, huge, sharp, dull, mean, angry, friendly, prickly, scaly, hard, soft, slimy, oily,* and *shiny*. Praise your child for good work and have fun catching what's in the ocean.

Things I Like

Cutting, pasting, and talking about pictures are fun activities your child will enjoy doing with you.

Playing the Activity: Give your child some colorful magazines. Ask him to cut out some of his favorite pictures and glue them on some paper. He might find and cut out pictures of vehicles, sporting events, foods, or toys. As he starts to glue the pictures on paper, talk about each one and ask him questions. If he cuts out a picture of a sailboat, ask, "Stevie, what is it?" and "Where does it go?" You may also ask, "Who rides on it?" and "Where do we find sailboats?" These questions will help you and your child start a conversation about sailboats.

Continue having your child cut and paste pictures. Ask him to talk to you about the different pictures he cuts out using descriptive words in complete sentences. Prompt him to ask you "wh" questions about his favorite pictures. Praise him for good talking and doing a terrific job.

Silly Stories

Surprise your child with some silly sentences during story time to see if she is really listening to you as you read.

Playing the Activity: Gather a few of your child's favorite story books such as *Snow White, Clifford the Dog,* or *Three Little Kittens.* Before you begin reading, remind your child to listen carefully because there are going to be a few silly surprises in the story. You can review the story a few times with your child to make sure she remembers important details about the story.

Next, tell your child to raise her hand when she hears something silly as you begin to read. Say, "Maddy, the three little kittens lost their whiskers and they began to yell." If she raises her hand, ask her to tell the story back to you using the correct words. If your child needs help, provide verbal cues and have her fill in some of the blanks as you read the sentence back to her. Say, "The three _____ lost their _____ and they began to _____." Give your child verbal praise for good listening and good work.

As you read, continue making silly sentences for your child to hear. Your child will enjoy listening to your silly stories and telling you that a few words are wrong and don't belong.

Talk and Listen

You will notice that your child's speech and language skills have become more advanced during the period of 4 to 5 years of age. Talking and listening to your child is the most positive way to reinforce your child's communication skills.

Playing the Activity: Talk with your child and make sure your child is talking to you. You can talk to your child anytime during regular daily routines. Say, "I'm loading dishes in the dishwasher," and "The dog needs some more food in his dog bowl." You can also say, "I am going to take the dog for a walk outside." Just talk, talk, and talk.

Make sure that your child is talking too. He can describe what he is doing during any of his daily routines. He can also ask you questions about what you are doing. Daily routines provide excellent opportunities for you and your child to engage in conversation. As he is describing what he is doing, help him build longer sentences by adding more and more words. You can describe what your child is doing too. Say, "I like how you are cleaning your room. You are doing a great job cleaning up your toys." Make sure you talk and ask questions at a level that is similar to your child's age. Don't hesitate to repeat, expand, and add more words onto your child's responses.

Also, during story time have your child pick out his favorite books. Sit and read to your child. Let your child use his imagination. Prompt him to talk in sentences and ask questions about everything he sees and hears using descriptive vocabulary words.

Finally, keep on talking to each other and take advantage of daily experiences that allow your child to express, use, and learn language.

Strategies for Developing Speech & Language Skills

- Use an encouraging tone when talking with your infant. Make good eye contact, smile back, and listen to your baby.
- Clearly pronounce sounds or true words when communicating with your child.
- Repeat and expand on your child's sounds or utterances that you hear your child produce (e.g., "baba, bottle; Yes, it is your bottle").
- Encourage your child to express his wants, needs, or feelings (e.g., "Tommy, tell me about your day").
- Talk to your child about what you are doing. This is called "self talk" and allows your child to understand that words match with objects and events.
- Ask "wh" questions (e.g., what, where, when, why) to help your child recall and retain details related to a topic of discussion.
- Add new information to help your child produce longer utterances or simple sentences (e.g., Child says, "Bird fly." You can say, "Yes, the bird is flying" or "Yes, the bird is flying in the sky").
- Comment on what your child is doing while he or she is playing. This is called "parallel talk" and requires parents or caregivers to describe out loud what their

child is looking at, listening to, or doing as he or she engages in playtime or daily activities.

- Look at picture books and read stories to your child. Prompt your child to point to and talk about pictures using words, phrases, and sentences. Ask questions about what you have read and have your child retell the story using his own words.
- Talk and listen to your child during daily routines and activities. This is the most positive way to reinforce your child's speech and language skills. Daily experiences provide your child with an enjoyable opportunity to learn and use language.

Index

Made in the USA
Middletown, DE
14 April 2022

64264757R00076